The Healing H Of The Zodiac

By Ada Muir

Distributed by:
W. FOULSHAM & CO. LTD.,
YEOVIL ROAD, SLOUGH, SL1 4JH ENGLAND

International Standard Book Number: 0-87542-120-2

First Edition, 1959
First Printing, 1959
Second Edition, 1974
Third Edition, 1985
Fourth Edition, 1986
First Printing, 1986
Second Printing, 1988

Cover Drawing: Nancy Benson

Produced by Llewellyn Publications
Typography and Art property of Chester-Kent, Inc.

Published by
LLEWELLYN PUBLICATIONS
A Division of Chester-Kent, Inc.
P.O. Box 64383
St. Paul, MN 55164-0383, U.S.A.

Printed in the United States of America

And God said
behold I have given you every herb bearing seed,
which is upon the face of all the earth, and every tree
in which is the fruit of a tree yielding seed;
to you it shall be for meat.
Genesis 1:29

And the fruit thereof shall be for meat
and the leaf thereof for medicine.
Ezekial 47:12

He causeth the grass to grow for cattle
and herbs for the use of man.
Psalm 104:14

For one believeth he may eat all things;
another who is weak eateth herbs.
Romans 14:2

And the leaves of the tree were for the healing of nations.
Revelation 22:2

Works by Ada Muir

The Book of Nodes and Part of Fortune
Cancer, Its Cause, Prevention and Cure
The Degrees of the Zodiac Analyzed
Food in Relation to Health
The Healing Herbs of the Zodiac
Health and the Sun Sign
Pluto: The Redeemer
The Sons of Jacob: A Study in Esoteric Astrology

Table Of Contents

Marjoram

The Healing Herbs Of The Zodiac

Introduction

Dating from Hippocrates who wrote in 460 B.C. and who is recognized as the founder of the art of healing, the properties and values of every wayside herb, tree and shrub have been known.

It was formerly the duty of every man studying the art of medicine, to be able to recognize every plant, understand its virtues, its Zodiacal sign and Planetary ruler and see that it was gathered under the most favourable planetary conditions.

Nowadays the herbalist knows nothing of this, except in a few cases, but he studies the properties of herbs from his

Winter Cress

1

textbook and applies them according to the symptoms of disease in his patients; and in this way is in danger of making as many mistakes in diagnosis and treatment as the medical man.

To give one instance, a friend was made very sick after taking a herbal compound containing barberry, an Aries herb. This had been very successful in the treatment of others suffering similarly, but the cause of the failure in her case was that Jupiter was her afflicting planet and she needed only those herbs in harmony with Jupiter.

To give her a Martial herb only intensified the complaint just as adverse aspects between Mars and Jupiter in a birth chart indicate intensity.

Then herbalists, in their compounding of herbs, often combine them irrespective of planetary laws and the active principal of one will counteract the active principal of another, which, if not injurious, is to say the least, wasteful.

The underlying cause of every disease is indicated in the birth chart as well as the weakness and strength of every

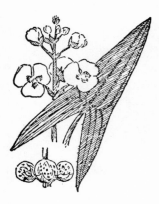

Arrow Head

organ of the body; for each of the twelve houses of the birth chart governs a definite part of the body.

The study of the Zodiacal rulership of plant life is an introduction to the study of medical astrology and as such should be of great assistance to students of that branch of the science.

Speedwell

Salad Burnet

Hyacinth

Centaury

The Herbs of Aries

The first house of the horoscope is ruled by Aries and since this describes the head and face in Natal astrology, it follows that the complaints of Aries are primarily complaints of the head and face.

The Sun enters Aries on March 20th and leaves it on April 20th each year. Mars is the planetary ruler of Aries, so those born while the Sun is in Aries, especially if born in the morning, display the Martial characteristics of desiring to rule and lead.

The complaints of Aries are of an inflammatory or feverish type, the most common being headache,

Honeysuckle

5

toothache, neuralgia, gum-boils, ringworm, smallpox (not the modern form of this disease, which is best designated as pimple-pox), mumps, polypus and burns or scars on the head and face.

The herbs of Mars, (the planetary ruler), being fiery, will help in some cases on the principle that fire will drive out fire by consuming everything inflammable.

It is also true that a fire may be extinguished rather than burned out and so, in some instances, it is better to use the soothing Venus herbs or the cooling and contracting Saturnine herbs, of which more will be said later.

Of the herbs of Aries, the best known are:

Hops: is especially good for sleeplessness, used either in a pillow stuffed with the bloom, and sleeping upon it, or as a tea, which should be drunk at bedtime. As a wash for ringworm and scabs on the head, it has no equal. It can also be made into an ointment and used for similar complaints.

Nettles: will check the flow of blood, is useful as a gargle for a sore mouth, and will stop the nose bleeding, either by

Holy Thistle

snuffing the dried powdered herb up the nostrils or using as a tea. It is a good spring tonic and blood-purifier.

Gentian: is well known as an appetizer and tonic, but it may also be used in the same way as hops. As a tea, it is a blood-purifier; wounds bathed with it are cleansed and healed.

Cayenne: is an excellent cure for nosebleeding, taken as a tea. Mixed with sage it is a remedy for nervous headache.

Broom Tea: is good as a cure for headache, and the green juice will cure toothache. If made into an ointment and rubbed well into the scalp it assists the growth of hair. It should not be used if Mars and Jupiter are afflicted.

Garlic: is valuable for treating pains in the ears. For this purpose the expressed juice is placed in the ears. As a poultice, garlic is excellent for the treatment of swellings.

Honeysuckle: made into an ointment, is good for massaging the back of the neck in cases of nervous headache, neuralgia and itch.

Blessed Thistle: is one of the best Aries and Mars plants.

Bistort

7

Used as a tea, it will relieve giddiness and swimming pains in the head, clear the blood, improve the complexion, and relieve ringworm and itch. It strengthens the memory, and is valuable as a relief for deafness.

For Astrological Students

While each Zodiacal Sign gives a general idea of the disease, the interplanetary vibrations give a more particular indication. For instance, in Aries subjects, if Mars is afflicted with Mercury, headaches and neuralgic pains are experienced and a nervine such as hops will give relief.

Mars and Venus afflicted incline towards bad habits and scrofulous disease and, for those, cleansing and antiseptic Venus herbs, or the cooling herbs of Saturn, are best.

Mars and Jupiter indicate a disordered liver and here the Jupiter herbs, or those under the rulership of Sagittarius or Pisces must be used.

Mars and the Sun induce fever and either Martial or Venus herbs are useful here.

Bog Myrtle

Mars and Saturn give rheumatic afflictions and the herbs of Mars will stimulate.

Mars and Neptune give disturbances of the astral fluids, as well as scrofulous complaints, and here Mars and Venus herbs combined will give relief.

*   *   *

Ill health is an indication of self-limitations.

The signs of the Zodiac give the history of these limitations as they tell of personal bias, fluctuating emotions, unruly desires and wandering thoughts.

The healing herbs of the Zodiac will modify physical conditions, but if the inner cause of the physical condition is understood and character strengthened at the same time, relief will be permanent.

*   *   *

The Desires of The Past are responsible for present

Broom

9

planetary aspects in our birth charts, as well as for our physical limitations.

The Desires of The Present are ever making our future horoscopes. We can purify these if we will, for we are each a ray from the Heart of all things, and always free to choose our thoughts—the makers of our destiny.

Gentian

The Herbs of Taurus

The second house of the Zodiac, the house of possessions, is ruled by Taurus, and this sign rules the neck and throat, so that the complaints of Taurus are primarily complaints of the neck and throat.

The Sun enters Taurus on April 20th and leaves about May 20th. Venus is the planetary ruler. Those born in the morning during that period display the Venusian characteristics of desiring to possess and protect their possessions.

The complaints of Taurus are due to excesses, often of an emotional nature, but sometimes over-indulgence in

Thyme

11

eating and drinking. The most common are scrofula or King's evil, wens, sore throat, quinsy, abscesses, enlarged tonsils, ague, goiter and bronchial afflictions.

The herbs of Venus purify the blood and keep the sweat glands open, thus allowing the poisonous ferments which have been generated in the body through excesses, emotionally or otherwise, to leave the body through the skin.

Sage: is the best known and probably the most valuable of the Taurus herbs. A tea made from it will allay emotional excitement, and dizziness. Mixed with vinegar, it is a gargle for sore throats. It will relieve quinsy and ulcerated throats, and is one of the best remedies for the mother who wishes to wean her baby, as it prevents food being converted into milk. It strengthens the nervous system and is said to lengthen life.

Dose: A teaspoonful in a half-pint of water. Steep for 24 hours but do not boil. Drink a teacup full night and morning.

Plantain

Thyme: is good for hysteria and is said to inspire courage. It is best used for flavouring for soups or salads.

Plantain: made into an ointment is a remedy for scrofula or King's evil.

Coltsfoot: is good for hoarseness, coughs and colds. One ounce to one pint of water, sweetened with honey. It will relieve scrofula if taken freely.

Tansy: will break up a cold if taken at bedtime, as it causes perspiration. The flowers, dried powdered and mixed with honey, will destroy worms. It is good for those suffering from periodical throat affections.

Silverweed: sweetened with honey, is an excellent gargle for weak and sore throats. Used as a tea it will relieve ague, as it drives the excess water out of the blood.

Goldenrod: applied outward, either as an ointment or poultice, will heal ulcers and, as a drink will heal ulcers in the mouth and throat. It is an excellent tonic for the gums, used strong as a wash or weaker as a drink.

Bearberry (Uva Ursi): has no equal for chronic throat

Tansy

13

affections. The bark should be soaked in water and, as it draws the strength out should be poured off and drunk; fresh water being then added until the bark gives off no further strength.

For Astrological Students

While the zodiacal signs give a general idea of the disease, the interplanetary vibrations give a more specialized indication. For instance, in Taurus subjects, if Venus is afflicted with Mars, scrofulous complaints through bad habits or contamination with others so afflicted will be the result. Outward and inward applications of Taurus herbs will be necessary to effect a cure.

Venus afflicted with Mercury by progression will result in neurasthenia and a combination of Taurus and Gemini herbs will give relief, or Taurus herbs alone.

Venus afflicted with the Moon will incline towards periodical ulcerations of the throat, and sage tea will remedy this.

Silverweed

14

Venus afflicted with the Sun by progression inclines to sore throat and watery discharges from the nostrils. A Taurus herb will be necessary.

Venus afflicted with Saturn inclines towards ague and chills, and a Martial and Taurus herb should be combined.

Venus afflicted with Jupiter inclines towards excesses, and a fruit fast will be best, combined with a Venus or Jupiter herb.

Venus afflicted with Uranus brings strange nervous disorders, sometimes induced by inoculations. Mercury and Taurus herbs will be necessary.

Venus afflicted with Neptune gives disorders of a neurotic type. A combination of Taurus and Aries herbs will be required, to cleanse and, at the same time, render the body more positive.

Colt's Foot

Cinquefoil   *Knotted Figwort*   *Heather*

The Herbs of Gemini

The third house of the horoscope is ruled by Gemini and describes the arms and breathing power; and since it is the house of the thinking ability, it also describes the nervous system, for on the quality of our thoughts depends the health of the nervous system.

The Sun enters Gemini on May 21st and leaves it on June 21st.

Mercury is the planetary ruler and those born when the Sun is in Gemini, especially during the morning hours, display the Mercurial characteristics of the message bearer and are usually quick and versatile thinkers.

Meadowsweet

17

The complaints of Gemini are bronchial affections, neuritis in the arms and shoulders, and nervous debility. Blood impurities and brain fevers are also Gemini complaints, the former resulting from insufficient breathing or foul atmosphere and the latter from lack of mental control or excessive study.

The best known herbs of Gemini are:

Skullcap: which is good for all complaints arising from nervous excitability, such as fits, convulsions, delirium tremens, St. Vitus' dance, neuritis and neuralgia. A quart of water to one ounce makes it the required strength and it should be drunk at night, and in extreme cases, every four hours during the day.

Lily of The Valley: is not so well known for its medicinal properties but it is useful in nervous disorders and the expressed juice will strengthen the eyes which are weakened through mental strain or study. When fright takes away the speech, this is restored by the flowers of this herb boiled in wine.

Flax or **Linseed Tea:** is well known since it is one of the

Skullcap

oldest remedies for coughs, the usual method of preparing being to boil it with liquorice and lemon. It is soothing to the bronchials and eaten raw is one of the finest laxatives. The expressed oil, used externally, relieves asthma.

Parsley: is used as a flavouring only, but is a nervine and blood purifier. It relieves inflamed eyes, when worry or study is the cause. As a tea, it is soothing and healing to people of Gemini type.

Ferns, Meadowsweet, Caraway and **Lavender** are under the rulership of Mercury and Gemini.

For Astrological Students

While each sign will give the predisposition to disease, interplanetary vibrations will give a more particular indication.

In the Gemini type, Mercury afflicted with Venus, by progression, has a powerful effect upon the mind, keying the nervous system to a high emotional pitch sometimes amounting to insanity. Any nervines except Valerian will help.

Viper's Bugloss

19

Mercury afflicted with Mars leads to nervous prostration, neuralgia and neuritis. The herbs of Mars will be necessary as a stimulant and tonic, as well as the nervines of Mercury.

Mercury afflicted with Jupiter leads to blood impurities. Jupiter herbs will be best.

Mercury afflicted with Saturn will require the harmonizing Venus herbs, as well as nervines.

Mercury afflicted with the Moon requires nervines and tonics.

Mercury afflicted with the Sun by progression affects eye-sight, which will be helped by herbs of the Sun.

Mercury afflicted by Uranus causes mental worry and nervines are necessary.

Mercury afflicted with Neptune causes a chaotic mental condition and nervines, as well as tonics, are necessary.

Flax

The Herbs of Cancer

The fourth house of the horoscope is ruled by Cancer and as this house describes the stomach and mammary glands, so the complaints of Cancer are very closely connected with the stomach and breast.

The Sun enters Cancer about June 22nd and leaves it about July 22nd. The Moon is the planetary ruler and those born while the Sun is passing through the sign are, like the Moon, reflective, changeable, orderly, adaptive yet defensive.

Just as the Moon reflects its surroundings so are its

Butterbur

subjects easily influenced by and susceptible to their surroundings.

The complaints of Cancer are indigestion and all weaknesses of the breast, chest and stomach, cancerous growths, dropsy, asthma and pleurisy.

The herbs of the planetary ruler will often help, but as the Cancer subject is so negative when ailing, the more stimulating herbs of one of the other signs often should be used.

The best known herbs of Cancer are:

Water Lily: is good for an ulcerated stomach but must be used carefully. It is most valuable as a wash for external ulcers. The juice from the flowers will remove freckles and sunburn.

Chickweed: an ointment made from this is excellent for erysipelas. It enters largely into the herbal remedies for obesity. As a poultice it is good for ulcerous sores and as a tea it will relive an ulcerated stomach.

Honeysuckle: one of the best remedies for stomach cramps, the leaves only being used.

Polypody

Dog's Tooth Violet: its expressed juice is good for dropsy, the leaves are cooling and healing if placed on ulcerous growths and the root, simmered in milk will remove stomach worms and relieve an ulcerated stomach.

Lettuce: is also a Cancer plant and its soothing sedative properties are well known.

For Astrological Students

The sign position and relationship of the Moon to other planets is very important in judging the Cancer predisposition to disease.

To give the inner meaning of each sign separately would take too much space here, but sign and house indicate the prevailing thoughts and on these health depends.

Interplanetary vibrations intensify thought in various directions and lead to inharmony and ill health.

Moon afflicting Sun affects eyesight and leads to spasmodic affections and cramps. Cancer and Leo herbs should be combined.

Violet

23

Ground Ivy

Moon afflicting Venus inclines towards sagging of the inter-cellular tissues and cancer, dropsy and varicose veins often result.

Moon afflicting Mercury induces nervous disorders and Gemini or Virgo herbs will be best.

Moon afflicting Mars gives an overheated blood stream and the cooling Saturnine herbs or herbs of Venus should be used.

Moon afflicting Jupiter inclines towards impurities of the blood leading to boils, pimples, eruptive diseases. Sagittarius and Cancer herbs should be combined to combat this.

Moon afflicting Saturn gives chills and colds that require Martial tonics.

Moon afflicting Uranus inclines towards nervous disorders which can be overcome by nervines and tonics. Avoid the herbs of Mars as these are over-stimulating.

Moon afflicting Neptune will affect in a similar manner to Venus except that there is also a nervous or neurotic condition The herbs of Mercury will help.

The Herbs of Leo

The fifth house of the horoscope, the house of children, speculation, education and pleasure, is ruled by Leo, and this sign governs the heart and arterial circulation.

The Sun enters Leo on July 23rd and leaves it August 23rd. The Sun is the planetary ruler of the sign and those born in the morning during this period display the Sun characteristics of faith, optimism and the desire to rule and lead. Just as the Sun is the centre of our universe so they aim to be the centre of their circle of acquaintances.

The complaints of Leo are heart affections, convulsions,

St. John's Wort

pleurisy, palpitation, inflammatory fever, jaundice, sore eyes, cramp and spasms.

The herbs of Leo strengthen the eyes, equalize the circulation and relieve spasmodic affections.

The most important of them are:

Eyebright: is used as a wash for inflamed eyes. It may also be used internally and is good for coughs, colds, ear-ache and headache. If taken before breakfast, it is good for epilepsy.

St. John's Wort: is one of the best remedies for asthma. Externally it is used as an ointment for dispelling tumours.

Mistletoe: is a tonic and stimulant for a nervous heart. It is good for convulsive fits, palsy and vertigo.

Marigold: is a remedy for sore eyes, especially during measles. The juice is said to remove warts.

Wake Robin: is a remedy for asthma, the root, bruised or pulverized being used, sweetened with honey.

Walnuts: are one of the finest Leo foods and should be added to every salad, whether fruit or vegetable.

Eyebright

26

For Astrological Students

Interplanetary relationships between the Sun and other planets chiefly affect arterial circulation with its attendant evils.

Sun and Moon afflicted affects eyesight. Herbs of the Sun will give tone and strength.

Sun and Mercury by parallel or progression incline towards fear and nervous heart. Mecurial herbs will be best.

Sun and Venus by parallel or progression tend towards sluggish circulation. Stimulating Leo or Aries herbs will be best.

Sun and Mars overheat the blood and the cooling Venus or Saturn herbs should be used to counteract.

Sun and Jupiter affect the liver and eyesight. Avoid all Martial herbs. Venus, Jupiter and Sun herbs and food will help. Appetite should be controlled, and frequent fasts may be necessary.

Sun and Saturn afflicted give gouty and rheumatic

Mistletoe

complaints, and sudorific herbs of Venus will be necessary.

Sun and Uranus afflicted give deep-seated complaints of the nervous system. Mercurial and Sun herbs will help.

Sun and Neptune afflicted affect the astral fluid. Tonics and nervines will be necessary.

Sun afflicted with the Moon's Nodes will act like Sun and Saturn.

Marsh Marigold

The Herbs of Virgo

The sixth house of the horoscope, the house which governs voluntary service, is ruled by Virgo, the sign which governs liver, solar plexus and the intestines.

The Sun enters Virgo on August 23rd and leaves it on September 23rd. Mercury is the planetary ruler and those born in the morning during this period, display the Mercurial characteristics of discrimination and love of scientific research, or, in less advanced types, criticism and fault-finding.

The complaints of Virgo are dysentry, obstructions in the bowels, intestinal worms, colic gastritis, nervous

Blue Flag

29

disorders, appendicitis. The organ mainly responsible for this is the liver, the physical seat of responsibility.

The herbs of Virgo must nourish the liver and educate it back to normal activity, soothe the nervous system, allay fear and heal the intestinal tract.

Skullcap: will tone the nervous sytem, strengthen the solar plexus, the seat of fear.

Fennel: will counteract flatulency. Dill will cleanse the digestive tract of ulcerations. Mandrake is a powerful liver cleanser, but should be used sparingly and with other herbs of a milder nature. It is one of the best agents, properly used, for cancerous conditions of the blood stream.

Licorice: sweetens the blood and reduces fever in the intestines. Endive cools the liver and allays inflammation. Pillitory of the Wall removes obstructions of the liver. Added to marshmallow and made into an ointment it will cleanse and heal fistulas.

Marshmallow

For Astrological Students

While each zodiacal sign gives a general idea of the part

of the body likely to be affected, interplanetary vibrations give a more particular indication.

In Virgo subjects, the sign and aspects of Mercury as well as afflictions from the other Common signs, will give the history of liver disturbances, and on the healthy activity of the liver depends the health of the solar plexus and intestines, as well as the nervous system generally.

Mercury afflicted with Mars calls for Mercurial and Venus herbs. Liver tonics must be avoided until the over-acidity resulting from that planetary combination has been checked.

Mercury afflicted with the Sun requires the herbs of Leo to eliminate eye-strain.

Mercury afflicted with the Moon can be helped by nervines and Cancer herbs.

Mercury afflicted with Jupiter requires the alternatives of Sagittarius and nervines of Virgo combined, but avoid the herbs of Mars.

Mercury afflicted with Saturn induces nervous strain and the soothing Venus herbs combined with nervines will help.

Cranesbill

31

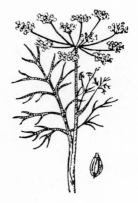

Fennel

Mercury afflicted with Uranus inclines towards extreme nervous affections.

Nervines and demulcents should be combined.

Mercury afflicted with Venus and Neptune excites the nervous system. Venus and Mercury herbs will relieve.

Whenever Mercury is afflicted, the nerve fluids are affected and the various nerve centres of the body are congested.

Nervines must be used as well as laxatives, for nervines by themselves tend towards constipating the bowels.

Nervines and laxatives can be combined without one reducing the effect of the other.

The Herbs of Libra

The seventh house of the horoscope, the house of marriage and business partners, is ruled by Libra, the sign which governs the kidneys, the seat of domestic harmony.

The Sun enters Libra September 23rd and leaves it October 23rd. Those born in the morning during this period display the Venus-Libra characteristics of desiring the association of others. In less advanced types partnerships are quickly formed and broken, approbativeness being the strongest trait.

The complaints of Libra are gravel, stone, pains in the back. inflammation of the kidneys and bladder, general

Archangel

33

debility. Libra is one of the most important signs in the horoscope for on this, wherever is is placed, depends our poise and balance.

When there are afflictions from the sign Libra, the blood loses its alkaline properties and a physical condition known as over-acidity results. This affects the stomach causing flatulency, affects the sweat glands, causing unpleasant body odours, weakens the kidneys leading to various forms of kidney disease and finally affects the lower brain leading to hallucinations and insanity.

The herbs of Libra then must tone the kidneys, keep the pores of the skin active that the daily load of carbonaceous waste material may be lessened and restore the sodium phosphate, the mineral salt which helps to maintain the balance between acids and alkalis.

Some of the herbs of Libra are to be found in every district where human life is possible, the following being the most common:

Pennyroyal: is warming and soothing. Many mothers use

Burdock

a weak tea of this herb for feverish, teething babies.

Violet: is recognized as a remedy for internal and external cancer, a disease condition which always indicates lack of the phosphates.

It has a cooling effect on the kidneys and is a remedy for scalding urine.

Thyme: is excellent for headaches and giddiness arising from nervous kidneys.

Feverfew: will strengthen and cleanse the kidneys.

Catmint: is similar to Pennyroyal and Feverfew in its action.

Silver Weed: is useful where there is over-activity of the kidneys but this should be used cautiously and combined with a herb of an emollient nature.

Archangel: will open the pores of the skin.

Bearberry: is a kidney tonic but should be used only with the milder herbs.

Burdock: may be safely used in all forms of kidney weakness.

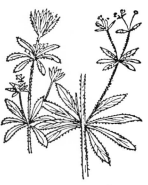

Cleavers

For Astrological Students

Interplanetary vibrations are very important in considering the health condition of the Libra type. We have here involved the planets of Venus, Saturn, Mars and the Moon, which are intimately associated with home and honour, and on these depend the healthy activity of the kidneys.

Venus afflicted with Mars increases sensitiveness to criticism, which leads to nervous breakdowns and sometimes depravity in various forms. The herbs of Mars or Venus will help. Saturn's herbs may be used alone.

Venus afflicted with Mercury often weakens the moral fibre. Mercurial herbs will give tone to the nerves.

Venus afflicted with the Moon affects the glandular system. The tonics of Mars with the sudorifics of Venus will help.

Venus afflicted with the Sun by progression causes chills. Sun herbs will assist.

Venus afflicted by Saturn affects sex organs, often

Butcher's Broom

36

leading to moral depravity. Saturnine herbs will be most useful in reducing inflammatory conditions.

Venus afflicted by Uranus is similar in effect to Mercurial afflictions. Nervines will be most useful.

Venus afflicted with Neptune disturbs the astral fluids and so leads to distorted imagination. Mars and Sun herbs will stimulate. Venus herbs are also necessary.

Pennyroyal

Water Horehound   *Periwinkle*   *Eupatorium*

The Herbs of Scorpio

The eighth house of the horoscope, the house of possessions of partners, is ruled by Scorpio, and this sign governs the generative organs.

The Sun enters Scorpio on October 23rd and leaves it November 22nd. Mars is the planetary ruler and those born in the morning during this period display the Martial characteristics of self-confidence, energy and activity and, in less evolved types, pride, vanity and passion.

The complaints of Scorpio are secret diseases connected with the generative organs, ruptures, piles, uterine troubles, catarrh of the bladder, etc.

Toad Flax

39

The herbs of Scorpio are cleansing and antiseptic, forcing impurities to leave the body through their natural channels—the bladder, intestines and skin.

The best known are **horehound**, **blackberry leaves**, **blessed thistle**, **horse radish**, **toad-flax**, **leek**, **wormwood** and sarsaparilla, all of which have antiseptic, healing properties, stimulating the glandular system that it may throw off the poisonous wastes which may otherwise accumulate in throat, bladder or generative organs, causing serious inflammatory disorders.

For Astrological Students

The position and apsects of Mars should be carefully noted in the health study of the Scorpio type.

Mars elevated often gives a very strong constitution but if afflicted, complaints are very sudden, deep-seated and complicated.

Mars afflicted with Neptune inclines towards neurotic thoughts and actions. Cooling Saturnine herbs will be best.

Wormwood

Mars afflicted with Uranus inclines towards nervous, feverish complaints. Gemini herbs should be used.

Mars afflicted with Saturn gives rheumatic tendencies. Venus herbs will give best results.

Mars afflicted with Venus is similar to Neptune.

Mars afflicted with Mercury produces nervous disorders and should be treated with Martial and Mercurian herbs.

Mars afflicted with the Sun overheats the blood and Leo and Venus herbs will remedy.

Mars afflicted with the Moon will be similar in effect to Venus and Neptune.

Water Plantain

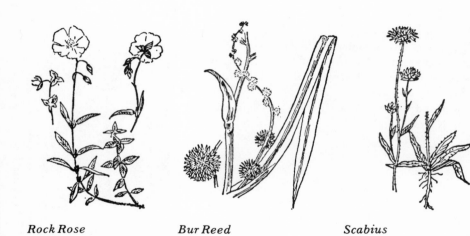

Rock Rose   *Bur Reed*   *Scabius*

The Herbs of Sagittarius

The ninth house of the horoscope, the house of philosophy, religion, law and long journeys, is ruled by Sagittarius, and this sign governs the thighs, the organs of locomotion.

The Sun enters Sagittarius on November 22nd and leaves it December 21st. Those born in the morning during this period display the optimistic characteristics of Jupiter and the desire to take chances in seeking new worlds to conquer, as well as new philosophies of life.

The complaints of Sagittarius are accidents through haste and violent exercise; feverish complaints through excesses and overheated blood, rheumatism and neuritis in

Solomon's Seal

the lower limbs and, since Jupiter endows many of its subjects with an inordinate amount of pride—and goiter is a disease of injured pride or humiliation—goiter may be classed as a Sagittarius complaint.

Some forms of cancer may also be classed as Sagittarius complaints, especially cancer of the liver and intestines; but where this is the case it will be found that Jupiter is afflicted in one of the Common signs.

The herbs of Sagittarius cool the blood, reduce fever and heal. The most important of them are:

Agimony: which will allay fever and tone the liver.

Red Clover: which is one of the most efficacious remedies for goiter.

Burdock: which is cooling and purifying to the blood stream.

Podophyllum or **May Apple:** has no equal in acting in and through the tissues, cleansing, healing and purifying. It is one of the best herbs for internal cancer.

Chicory: is good for liver impurities, which result from over-heated blood.

Agrimony

Dandelion: is a member of the chicory family and is of equal value in cleansing the overheated blood stream.

Oak: is one of the finest astringents and was used by many herbalists during smallpox epidemics as a preventative. The bark is boiled and the body bathed with the liquid. It is also used as a cure for goiter, the method being to soak a cloth in an oak bark solution each evening and wrap around the throat, covering with a dry cloth.

For Astrological Students

Jupiter, the ruler of Sagittarius, must be carefully studied as the house and sign for correct diagnosis of disease. For instance, Jupiter afflicted with the Moon will, in some cases, lead to obesity and, in others, lack of appetite.

Jupiter afflicted with Neptune or Venus is a frequent forerunner of goiter, and Jupiter herbs will relieve.

Jupiter afflicted with Saturn leads to sluggish action of the blood, ending in nervous prostration, neuritis and

Red Clover

45

rheumatism. Nervines combined with the herbs of Sagittarius should be used.

Jupiter adverse with Mercury causes headaches, dizziness and sometimes congestion of the brain. Nervines and Jupiter herbs should be used here.

Jupiter in affliction with the Sun sometimes leads to apoplexy, palpitation of the heart and the loss of sight of one eye, if in fixed signs. Jupiter herbs will be best but living must be abstemious.

Jupiter afflicted with Mars gives impure blood, diseases of the liver, liability to burns and accidents. Martial herbs should be avoided and, instead, the cooling, soothing Venus herbs used.

Jupiter afflicted with Uranus affects the nervous system and Jupiter and Gemini herbs should be used.

Chicory

The Herbs of Capricorn

The tenth house of the horoscope is ruled by Capricorn and describes the knees, bony structure and skin.

The Sun enters Capricorn on the 22nd of December and leaves it on the 20th of January.

Saturn is the planetary ruler and those born when the Sun is in Capricorn, especially during the morning hours, will display the Saturnine characteristics of ambition, diplomacy and tact or secretiveness and cunning.

The complaints of Capricorn are rheumatism of the knees and lower limbs, skin diseases, fractures, weak knees, leprosy, ruptures, rickets, corns and warts.

Comfrey

47

The best known herbs of Capricorn are:

Comfrey Root: is an excellent remedy for ruptures and skin complaints. It should be grown in every garden as it is more efficacious if used fresh. Used externally, the leaves or the expressed juice of them will reduce swellings and heal ruptures. An ointment made from the green root will cure warts.

Horse Tail or **Shave Grass:** will check internal hemorrhages and an ointment made from it will relieve inflammatory sores.

Knot Grass: dissolves phlegm, checks bleeding from the mouth and nose and the expressed juice will heal external wounds. It hastens the healing of broken joints and ruptures and the juice will stop running ears.

Slippery Elm: there is no finer food and medicine than this. It is cooling, healing and soothing for the entire digestive tract. It is the best and most nutritive baby's food as it strengthens the bony structure and allays inflammatory tendencies. It should be kept in every household.

Horse Tail

Thuja: is one of the best remedies for warts on any part of the body.

Shepherd's Purse: is similar in effect to Knot Grass.

Wintergreen: is a remedy for rheumatism in the joints.

Fumitory and **Thyme:** are also Capricorn herbs.

For Astrological Students

The stimulating herbs of Mars are efficacious for many Capricorn complaints but interplanetary action will sometimes indicate a need for a combination of other herbs.

Saturn and the Sun afflicted cause palpitation of the heart, paralysis, sore eyes and cataracts. Leo herbs are best, combined with Slippery Elm. Thuja will relieve sore eyes and sometimes take away cataracts.

Saturn and Jupiter afflicted incline towards ruptures and Comfrey Root will be best.

Saturn and Mars also incline towards ruptures, rheumatism, mucous in the throat and deafness. Martial

Shepherd's Purse

49

herbs combined with Slippery Elm should be used.

Saturn and the Moon afflicted induce cold and flatulent complaints. Martial herbs will be best.

Saturn and Mercury induce nervous debility and affect the solar plexus. The herbs of the Sun and Mercury will give the best results.

Saturn and Venus incline towards diseases of the generative organs and lingering inflammatory and skin diseases. Slippery Elm and Venus or Martial herbs should be used.

Saturn and Neptune are similar to the above.

Saturn and Uranus seem to be sudden in their action but they give evidence of deep-seated complaints involving the nervous and renal system. These require stimulating and nervine herbs. Sage and Skullcap will benefit.

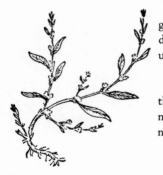

Knot Grass

The Herbs of Aquarius

The eleventh house of the horoscope is ruled by Aquarius and describes the condition of the calf and ankles. Aquarius also affects the blood stream through sympathy with Leo, its opposite sign, which rules the arterial circulation.

The Sun enters Aquarius about the 20th of January and leaves it on February 19th.

Uranus is the planetary ruler and those born when the Sun is in Aquarius, especially during the morning hours, display the Uranian characteristics of eccentricity and wilfulness, until they recognize their life work and are attached to either a person or a cause.

Ragwort

51

Restriction in any form is irritating to the Aquarian, yet, paradoxical as it may seem, inwardly they crave discipline.

This probably accounts for so many of them entering some form of government service, especially where a uniform is worn, such as in the army, navy, hospitals, asylums or prisons.

Later in life they recognize that self-discipline is the only real discipline. Then they realize that physical and mental control result in a healthy body.

The complaints of Aquarius are cramps in the calf of the leg, milk leg, rheumatic fever, blood impurities and paralysis. Since the sign is opposite Leo, the Sun Sign which rules one eye—the right in a man and left in a woman—the eyes are often affected.

The best known herbs of Aquarius are Valerian or Lady's Slipper. This may be used in hysteria, and delirium, as it quiets the nerves, allays pain and promotes sleep. One quart of water is used to one ounce of the herb powdered.

One of the worst cases we have known of epilepsy was cured by the use of this herb, but it should be used

All Heal

carefully as, in some cases, it over-stimulates the brain, thus increasing rather than decreasing the trouble.

Snake Root: also known as Spotted Plantain, is most useful as a wash for inflamed eyes, although it may be used internally and will remedy cramp in the legs.

Southernwood: popularly known as Old Man, is a remedy for hysteria.

The herbs of Leo are a great help in Aquarian complaints, especially in removing the cause of hysteria and cramp.

For Astrological Students

While each sign will give an idea of the predisposition to disease the interplanetary vibrations give a more particular indication.

In the Aquarian, Uranus afflicted with Mercury inclines to mental disorders and confusion. Such nervines as Valerian, in small doses will give relief in young people.

There is usually, however, a deep-seated cause when this

Wood Sage

53

planetary combination makes itself felt in later life, usually traceable to sex abuse. In mild cases hallucination or obsession will be noticed but in advanced cases, insanity requiring restraint will result.

To overcome this condition, the whole chart must be examined and the habits enquired into. Harmonizing Venus herbs will help. Stimulating Martial herbs sometimes do good, but more often harm and the herbs of Uranus will help to induce restful sleep.

It is always necessary to see that the liver is active, as well as the intestines regular, before giving herbs of a nervine nature, for poisons from the intestinal tract merely intensify the complaint.

Uranus afflicted with Venus leads to sexual excesses owing to the magnetic stimulation through this planetary combination. Southernwood is one of the best tonics for women and sage tea for men where over-stimulation leads to neurotic thoughts.

Uranus afflicted with Mars leads to blood impurities through heat and impulsive thought and action. Uranian

Blue Vervain

54

and Jupiter herbs will help. Saturnine herbs will cool the blood stream and check any tendency towards apoplexy.

Uranus afflicted with Jupiter leads to blood impurities, and cooling laxative Jupiter herbs will be best.

Uranus afflicted with the Sun will induce cramps, nervous and hysterical conditions. Uranian and Sun herbs combined will give relief.

Uranus afflicted with the Moon causes hysteria, nervous complaints, weakened eyesight. Uranian herbs combined with those under the Moon should be used.

Uranus afflicted with Saturn induces cold, rheumatic and nervous disorders. The stimulating herbs of Mars will be useful here.

Uranus afflicted with Neptune will have a similar effect to the Venus and Mercurial afflictions and the same remedies apply.

Celandine

55

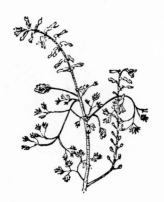  

Fumitory   *Mullein*   *Purple Loosetrife*

The Herbs of Pisces

The twelfth house of the horoscope is ruled by Pisces and, since this describes the condition of the feet, it follows that complaints of Pisces are primarily complaints of the feet and toes.

The Sun enters Pisces on February 19th and leaves it on March 20th. Neptune is the planetary ruler of Pisces, so those born while the Sun is passing through the sign display the Neptunian characteristics of pathos, winsomeness and sympathy—or selfishness and cunning—according to the degree of their development.

The complaints of Pisces are gout, boils, ulcers,

Bog Bean

abscesses, corns, bunions, enlarged feet, lameness, etc., arising from cold and moisture.

The herbs of the planetary ruler, Neptune, will help, but Pisces is a negative sign and so the stimulating Martial herbs are often necessary to inspire the courage which the sick Pisces subject often lacks.

Pisces has rulership over all sea-weeds, sea-water mosses and native water plants.

Irish Moss: is a valuable Pisces herb. It is often called Consumptive's Moss because it will relieve consumption. It should be soaked in water for twenty-four hours, then boiled in either milk or water.

If boiled in milk it can be used as a porridge. If boiled in water add fruit juice and allow to set, when it makes an excellent and nourishing invalid's jelly.

Most children relish Irish Moss if it is properly prepared, but for those who dislike it and cannot be persuaded to eat it as a porridge or jelly, it can be added to soups, where it is not noticed.

Yarrow

It contains iron and iodine in the only form in which these can be assimilated by the body.

An enterprising firm in the United States reduced the moss to a powder and sold it at a good profit under the name of Sea Lettuce—a suitable name, as it has the virtues of the lettuce plus the tonic qualities peculiar to itself.

If it is used persistently, Irish Moss will relieve practically every Pisces complaint and children raised upon it—for it is an economical food—will not be consumptive or goiter subjects.

For Astrological Students

In Pisces subjects, if Neptune and Mercury are afflicted, hallucinations are common, and a Martial nervine is necessary, as well as a Neptunian herb. Cayenne, hops, gentian or ginger, added to Irish Moss will provide a remedy.

Neptune and Venus incline to moral laxity, or afflictions

Woundwort

59

of the generative organs. Irish Moss added to a Venus herb will remedy.

Neptune and Jupiter afflicted create blood impurities so, for a remedy, add the Moss to a Jupiter herb.

Neptune and the Sun afflicted causes mental and emotional disturbances, and a Sun herb must be added to the Moss to effect a cure.

Neptune and Saturn produce cold and rheumatic diseases, which can be overcome by the stimulating Mars herbs used in conjunction with the herbs.

Neptune and Mars incline towards emotional excesses and, in such cases, a blood purifier is necessary, such as blood-root or sarsaparilla, Scorpian herbs.

Neptune and Uranus sometimes cause mental diseases and those herbs which act as nervines, added to the Moss, will give the best results.

Notice to Students—The Rising Sign, which can only be found when the exact time of birth is known, is the chief indicator of the constitution and, as correctives, herbs in

Borage

harmony with the Rising Sign should be chosen first.

The part of the body most liable to affliction will be the part governed by the rising sign and the sign of its planetary ruler. Signs containing planets which form aspects with the planetary ruler of the ascendant must also be considered.

Sun Dew

Index of Illustrations

STAY IN TOUCH

On the following pages you will find listed, with their current prices, some of the books and tapes now available on related subjects. Your book dealer stocks most of these, and will stock new titles in the Llewellyn series as they become available. We urge your patronage.

However, to obtain our full catalog, to keep informed of new titles as they are released and to benefit from informative articles and helpful news, you are invited to write for our bi-monthly news magazine/catalog. A sample copy is free, and it will continue coming to you at no cost as long as you are an active mail customer. Or you may keep it coming for a full year with a donation of just $2.00 in U.S.A. ($7.00 for Canada & Mexico, $20.00 overseas, first class mail). Many bookstores also have *The Llewellyn New Times10 available to their customers. Ask for it.*

Stay in touch! In The Llewellyn New Times' pages you will find news and reviews of new books, tapes and services, announcements of meetings and seminars, articles helpful to our readers, news of authors, advertising of products and services, special money-making opportunities, and much more.

The Llewellyn New Times
P.O. Box 64383-Dept. 486, St. Paul, MN 55164-0383, U.S.A.

• • •

TO ORDER BOOKS AND TAPES

If your book dealer does not have the books and tapes described on the following pages readily available, you may order them direct from the publisher by sending full price in U.S. funds, plus $1.00 for handling and 50 cents each book or item for postage within the United States; outside USA surface mail add $1.50 per item postage and $1.00 per order for handling. Outside USA air mail add $7.00 per item postage and $1.00 per order for handling. MN residents add 6% sales tax.

MAGICAL HERBALISM—The Secret Craft of the Wise
by Scott Cunningham

In Magical Herbalism, certain plants are prized for the special range of energies—the vibrations, or powers—they possess. Magical Herbalism unites the powers of plants and man to produce, and direct, change in accord with human will and desire.

This is the Magic of amulets and charms, sachets and herbal pillows, incenses and scented oils, simples and infusions and annointments. It's Magic as old as our knowledge of plants, an art that anyone can learn and practice, and once again enjoy as we look to the Earth to re-discover our roots and make inner connections with the world of Nature.

This is Magic that is beautiful and natural—a Craft of Hand and Mind merged with the Power and Glory of Nature: a special kind that does not use the medicinal powers of herbs, but rather the subtle vibrations and scents that touch the psychic centers and stir the astral field in which we live to work at the causal level behind the material world.

This is the Magic of Enchantment . . . of word and gesture to shape the images of mind and channel the energies of the herbs. It is a Magic for *everyone*—for the herbs are easily and readily obtained, the tools are familiar or easily made, and the technology that of home and garden.

This book includes step-by-step guidance to the preparation of herbs and to their compounding in incesnse and oils, sachets and amulets, simples and infusions, with simple rituals and spells for every purpose.

ISBN: 0-87542-120-2, 243 pgs., 5¼ x 8, illustrated, soft cover.   **$7.95**

CUNNINGHAM'S ENCYCLOPEDIA OF MAGICAL HERBS
by Scott Cunningham

This is an expansion on the material presented in his first Llewellyn book, *Magical Herbalism*. This is not just another herbal for medicinal uses of herbs; this is the most comprehensive source of herbal data for magical uses. Each of the over 400 herbs are illustrated and the magical properties, planetary rulerships, genders, deities, folk and latin names are given. There is a large annotated bibliography, a list of mail order suppliers, a folk name cross reference, and all the herbs are fully indexed. No other book like it exists. Find out what herbs to use for luck, love, success, money, divination, astral projection and much more. Fun, interesting and fully illustrated with unusual woodcuts from old herbals.

0-87542-122-9, 6 x 9, 350 pp., illustrated, softcover.   **$12.95**

EARTH POWER by Scott Cunningham

This is a book of folk magic—the magic of the common people. As such, it is different from nearly every other published work on the subject. This book is for the people of the Earth. The practices are so easy as placing a leaf in a north wind. The ritual is married to the forces of Nature. This is natural magic rediscovered. This book can not only help you learn these natural magical methods, but it can also put you in touch with the planet that nurtures you.

ISBN: 0-87542-121-0, 5¼ x 8, illustrated, softbound.   **$6.95**

COLOR MAGIC
by Raymond Buckland
The world is a rainbow of color, a symphony of vibration. We have left the Newtonian idea of the world as being made of large mechanical units, and now know it as a strange chaos of vibrations ordered by our senses, but, our senses are limited and designed by Nature to give us access to only those vibratory emanations we need for survival.

But, we live far from the natural world now. And the colors which filled our habitats when we were natural creatures have given way to grey and black and synthetic colors of limited wave lengths determined not by our physiological needs but by economic constraints.

Raymond Buckland, author of the world-famous PRACTICAL CANDLE BURNING RITUALS has produced a fascinating and useful new book, PRACTICAL GUIDE FOR COLOR MAGIC which shows you how to reintroduce color into your life to benefit your physical, mental and spiritual well-being!
- Learn the secret meanings of color.
- Use color to change the energy centers of your body.
- Heal yourself and others through light radiation.
- Discover the hidden aspects of your personality through color.

PRACTICAL COLOR MAGIC will teach all the powers of light and more! You'll learn new forms of expression of your inner-most self, new ways of relating to others with the secret languages of light and color. Put true color back into your life with the rich spectrum of ideas and practical magical formulas from COLOR MAGIC!
ISBN: 0-87542-047-8, 200 pp., illustrated   **$6.95**

PRACTICAL CANDLEBURNING RITUALS
by Raymond Buckland, Ph. D.

Another book in Llewellyn's Practical Magick series. Magick is a way in which to apply the full range of your hidden psychic powers to the problems we all face in daily life. We know that normally we use only 5% of our total powers—Magick taps powers from deep inside our psyche where we are in contact with the Universe's limitless resources.

Magick need not be complex—it can be as simple as using a few candles to focus your mind, a simple ritual to give direction to your desire, a few words to give expression to your wish.

This book shows you how easy it can be. Here is Magick for fun, Magick as a Craft, Magick for Success, Love, Luck, Money, Marriage, Healing; Magick to stop slander, to learn truth, to heal an unhappy marriage, to overcome a bad habit, to break up a love affair, etc.

Magick—with nothing fancier than ordinary candles, and the 28 rituals in this book (given in both Christian and Old Religion versions)—can transform your life. Illustrated.
ISBN: 0-87542-048-06, 189 pg., 5¼ x 8, softbound.   **$5.95**

THE LLEWELLYN ANNUALS

Llewellyn's MOON SIGN BOOK: approximately 400 pages of valuable information on gardening, fishing, weather, stock market forecasts, personal horoscopes, good planting dates, and general instructions for finding the best date to do just about anything! Articles by prominent forecasters and writers in the fields of gardening, astrology, politics, economics and cycles. This special almanac, different from any other, has been published annually since 1906. It's fun, informative and has been a great help to millions in their daily planning. **State year $3.95**

Llewellyn's SUN SIGN BOOK: Your personal horoscope for the entire year! All 12 signs are included in one handy book. Also included are political and economic forecasts, special feature articles, and lucky dates for each sign. Monthly horoscopes by a prominent radio and TV astrologer for your personal Sun Sign. Articles on a variety of subjects written by well-known astrologers from around the country. Much more than just a horoscope guide! Entertaining and fun the year round. **State year $3.95**

Llewellyn's DAILY PLANETARY GUIDE and ASTROLOGER'S DATEBOOK: Includes all of the major daily aspects plus their exact times in Eastern and Pacific time zones, lunar phases, signs and voids plus their times, planetary motion, a monthly ephemeris, sunrise and sunset tables, special articles on the planets, signs, aspects, a business guide, planetary hours, rulerships, and much more. Large 5¼ × 8 format for more writing space, spiral bound to lay flat, address and phone listings, time zone conversion chart and blank horoscope chart. **State year $6.95**

Llewellyn's ASTROLOGICAL CALENDAR: Large wall calendar of 52 pages. Beautiful full color cover and color inside. Includes special feature articles by famous astrologers, introductory information on astrology, Lunar Gardening Guide, celestial phenomena for the year, a blank horoscope chart for your own chart data, and monthly date pages which include aspects, lunar information, planetary motion, ephemeris, personal forecasts, lucky dates, planting and fishing dates, and more. 10 x 13 size. Set in Central time, with conversion table for other time zones worldwide. **State year $6.95**

THE GODDESS BOOK OF DAYS
by Diane Stein

Diane Stein has created this wonderful guide to the Goddesses and festivals for every day of the year! This beautifully illustrated perpetual datebook will give you a listing for every day of the special Goddesses associated with that date along with plenty of room for writing in your appointments. It is a hardbound book for longevity, and has over 100 illustrations of Goddesses from around the world and from every culture. This is sure to have a special place on your desk. None other like it!

0-87542-758-8, 300 pgs., hardbound, 5¼ x 8, illus. **$12.95**